Training for Kids

By
Kim Campbell Thornton
Illustrations by Buck Jones

Karla Austin, *Director of Operations and Product Development*
Nick Clemente, *Special Consultant*
Barbara Kimmel, *Editor in Chief*
Jessica Knott, *Production Supervisor*
Jimmie Young, *Layout Design*
Cover and book design concept by Michael V. Capozzi

Kim Campbell Thornton is an award-winning writer and editor. During her tenure as editor of *Dog Fancy*, the magazine won three Dog Writers Association of America Maxwell Awards for best all-breed magazine. Since beginning a new career in 1996 as a freelance writer, she has written or contributed to more than a dozen books about dogs and cats. Her book *Why Do Cats Do That?* was named best behavior book in 1997 by the Cat Writers' Association. The companion book *Why Do Dogs Do That?* was nominated for an award by the Dog Writers Association of America. Kim serves on the DWAA Board of Governors and on the board of the Dog Writers Educational Trust. She is also president of the Cat Writers' Association and belongs to the National Writers Union.

Buck Jones's humorous illustrations have appeared in numerous magazines (including *Dog Fancy* and *Cat Fancy*) and books. He is the illustrator for the best-selling books *Barking, Chewing, Digging, Kittens! Why Do They Do What They Do?* and *Puppies! Why Do They Do What They Do?*

The dogs in this book are referred to as *he* and *she* in alternating chapters.

ISBN: 978-1-933958-56-9

BowTie Press®
A Division of BowTie, Inc.
23172 Plaza Pointe Drive, Suite 230
Laguna Hills, California 92653

Printed and Bound in Malaysia
10 09 08   1 2 3 4 5 6 7 8 9 10

Contents

Introduction

Training a dog is more than teaching her to sit and stay. Training means teaching your dog not to go potty in the house, how to do what you ask, and how to be nice to people and other animals. If you want to do canine sports, you need to train your dog for those. Adults and older kids should be the main trainers, but younger kids can be great helpers. Never train your dog without an adult around.

You may think that training a dog is too much work or that dogs don't like it. The truth is that well-trained

dogs are less work and more fun. A trained dog can go with you to the park and to friends' houses. She will come when you call her. Dogs that aren't trained may feel afraid or unsure in new situations. They get into trouble a lot, but they aren't sure why you are mad. Untrained dogs are often tense and anxious, but a trained dog is relaxed and friendly.

First Things First: Crate- and House-Training

Teaching your dog not to potty in the house is called house-training. Crate-training is teaching your dog to sleep and relax in a crate. Dog crates are boxes made of wire or plastic with a door that opens in the front. Although a crate may look uncomfortable to you or me, dogs like them. Have you ever noticed that your dog likes to sleep under your bed or under a table or desk? The crate is like that except that you decide when your dog goes in and out of it. Crate-training and house-training go together like milk and cookies.

Crate-Training

Puppies are like babies; they get tired and fussy. The crate is a nice safe place for them to go when they need a nap. A crate is a good place for any dog to sleep and relax in at night and when you can't watch him. After a couple of days of crate-training,

your puppy will probably go into the crate on his own. Don't ever leave your dog or puppy in the crate for more than a few hours at a time during the day.

Your dog's crate must be just big enough for him to lie down, stand up, and turn around in. If the crate is too big for your dog, she may poop in one corner and sleep in the other! If you adopt a puppy, you'll probably end up buying two crates because you'll need a bigger one when he grows up. Or buy a crate with panels that can be used to make the crate bigger or smaller.

Teach your dog to love his crate as soon as he comes into your home. Put a cozy blanket in it so he

has something to snuggle up to. Give him a soft toy without any filling to snuggle with and a hard rubber toy to chew on. Don't give him rawhides, plush toys with filling, or bones while he is in his crate. He can rip these up and choke on them. He should play with these toys only when you are with him.

Introduce your pup to the crate slowly. Leave the door open. Let him sniff around the outside and inside. Put treats outside the crate, at the door of the crate and inside the crate, all the way to the back. Let him find them on his own and eat them. Do this three or four times.

Once your dog goes in and out of the crate by himself, shut the door quietly. Don't slam it because this will scare him. Feed him a few treats through the door, then open the door. Do this three or four times. Then, let him stay in the crate for a few minutes at a time. Stay with him and give him treats every once in a while. Increase the amount of time he stays in the crate. If he starts scratching at the door, whining, or barking, wait until he is quiet and calm. Then, let him out. Don't let him out right away when he whines and barks. He won't learn to relax in the crate if he thinks barking will make you let him out.

After your dog is comfortable in the crate with you nearby, leave him alone in the crate. The first time, leave the room for only a minute. Then leave the room for two minutes, three minutes, and so on. Once you can leave for ten minutes at a time, your dog is crate-trained! When you come back, you'll probably find him fast asleep or happily chewing on a toy.

Some dogs are crate-trained in an hour. For other dogs, it takes days or weeks of training before they are comfortable in the crate. Older dogs usually take more time than pups do. Be patient.

If you have had a puppy before and thought house-training was a big drag, you'll be surprised by how easy it is when you use a crate. House-training your dog is a lot easier than potty training your little sister or brother. And no one will have to change any diapers!

House-Training

There is only one rule to house-training: never let your puppy potty indoors. The trick to this is to never let your puppy out of your sight. Unless he is in his crate, he should be with someone at all times. That means your puppy should not wander around the house or be left in a room alone. When he isn't sleeping, playing, cuddling, eating, or chewing a toy in front of you, he should be in his crate. To remind yourself of this, keep your dog close by attaching his leash to your belt. That way you know he's always

nearby. (Younger kids shouldn't do this because an excited pup could pull them over!)

Why won't a puppy go potty in his crate? Dogs hate to sleep or relax in the same area where they go potty. If your puppy does pee or poop in his crate, he has probably been in there for too long or is sick.

Give your pup lots of chances to go potty outside. He needs to go potty at least every two hours. He also needs to go potty after playing, napping, and eating. Every time you take your pup out of his crate,

take him out to potty first thing. Take him outside after playing a game and after meals.

Learn the signs that your dog is getting ready to go potty. He will circle, sniff, and scratch at the floor when he is looking for a good spot. If you see him doing this, take him outside right away. If your puppy begins to squat or lift a leg in the house, say "No" and take your pup outside. Never yell at a dog for going potty in the house or rub his nose in the accident. This won't teach him anything except to be afraid of you.

Once your pup is outside, say "Go potty." When he does, say "Good boy." Do not play with your puppy until he goes potty. Potty breaks should be all business. If you and your family follow these instructions, your puppy may never have an accident in the house.

Training Equipment: Collars and Leashes

You need only two pieces of equipment to train your dog: a leather or nylon collar with a buckle, called a flat collar, and a six-foot leather or nylon leash with a small loop at one end and a clip at the other. Hold the loop in your left hand, and attach the clip to a ring on the dog's collar. The collar should be loose enough around your dog's neck that you can put two fingers beneath it, but not so loose that your dog can wriggle out of it. Now you can start training your dog.

How to Teach Commands

Every dog should know *come, sit, down, leave it, stay,* and how to walk nicely on a leash. Start teaching your dog as soon as you bring her home, whether she's an eight-week-old pup or a five-year-old adult.

Pay Attention

To get started, teach your pup to pay attention to you. This is fun and easy.

1. Show your dog you have a treat in your hand.
2. Say "Look at me." At first, your dog will look at your hand. Wait until she looks at your face. You may need to bring the treat up to your face the first couple of times.
3. When your dog looks at you, say "Good look at me" and give her a treat. Do this three or four times every day. Soon, your dog will look at you when you ask her to. If she's not really interested in treats, teach her to look at you with a squeaky toy. If she gets distracted

or walks away, show her the treat or toy again. If your dog is really distracted, you may need a partner to hold her on a leash while you show her the treats. Once your dog knows how to pay attention, you can start teaching her what she needs to know.

Sit

This is one of the commands you will use the most. Luckily, it's also one of the easiest to teach.

1. Stand in front of your dog with a treat in your hand.

2. Show your dog the treat, and hold it near her nose. Slowly move your hand in a straight line above her nose. She will raise her nose to follow the treat. As her nose goes up, her bottom will go down.

3. Once her nose is in the air and her bottom is on the ground, say "Good sit" and give her the treat. If she jumps up to follow the treat, wait until her front feet are on the floor before giving her the treat.

4. Repeat the exercise, but say "Sit" as you raise the treat. Once the bottom is down, say "Good sit" and give her the treat. Practice this at least ten times a day.

Down

Use *down* when you want your dog to lie down. It's a good command to use while you're eating dinner or when friends are over. You may need a partner to help you.

1. Stand in front of your dog and say "Sit."

2. When she sits, hold a treat in front of her nose. Slowly move the treat toward you to the ground. This will be a diagonal line from her nose to your feet. She will try to follow the treat, but she won't be able to reach it. To reach it, she must lie down.

3. When she lies down, say "Good down" and give her the treat. Some dogs will stand up to get the treat. If

your dog does this, ask a helper to gently hold her bottom down on the ground.

4. Once your dog is following the treat into the down position, add a command. This time, say "Down" as you lower the treat. Say "Good down" once she's lying down.

5. Practice this ten times a day.

6. Use a clicker to help practice this command. A clicker is a small metal box that makes a clicking sound when you press down on it. Any time you see your dog in the down position, even if you didn't ask her to do it, click once, say "Good down" and give her

a treat. Your dog learns that the "Click" sound means she's doing something right. When you say "Good down," it teaches her the word for what she's doing. You can use this trick to reinforce any command, from *roll over* to *sit*. Remember: click only once.

Stay

Stay means your dog stays in one place without moving. Teaching *stay* isn't as easy as teaching *sit* or *down*, but you can do it with practice.

1. Ask your dog to sit or lie down.
2. Stand in front of her and say "Stay." Put your hand out with the palm facing her as if you were telling someone to stop. Give her a treat. Do this several times.
3. Say "Stay," show her the palm of your hand, and wait five seconds before giving her a treat. If she stays for the five seconds, say "Good stay" and give her the treat. If she moves, put her back in position and start again. You may need a helper to do this. Do this five to ten times a day for three or four days.

4. After your dog stays for five seconds, have her stay for ten seconds, and so on. Once she stays for twenty seconds, take a step back and start over. Keep doing this until your dog stays even when you are across the room. Make it harder by adding distractions such as having a friend jump up and down, clap, or walk in front of your dog. You will probably need to do each step five to ten times for three or four days.

Come

This is the most important command your dog will learn. Use the *come* command when you want your dog

to run to you right away. If your dog doesn't know this, she could run away or be hit by a car.

We accidentally teach dogs NOT to come all the time. Here's what NOT to do:

1. Never chase your dog. Chasing your dog teaches her to run away from you.
2. If you ask your dog to come, make sure she does. That means keeping her on a leash so she won't run away until you know she will always come when you call.
3. Always give your dog praise or a treat when she comes. Never punish her when she comes, even if it took a long time for her to get to you!

4. Ask your dog to come for good reasons. Don't ask her to come only when you are leaving the park or you want to give her a bath. Call her and give her a quick butt rub or a treat.

To teach your dog TO come, follow these rules:

1. Teach your dog to come in your own yard first. When teaching the *come* command, always keep your dog on a leash. If she won't come to you, gently pull her to you by her leash.

2. Show your pup that you have a handful of really good treats. Run away from her, saying "Come Daisy" (or whatever her name is).

3. When she catches up to you, turn around and face her. Give her a treat and say "Good come." Do this at least ten times so your pup understands that she gets good treats every time she runs after you.

4. Ask a friend to hold your dog in place by her leash. Stand ten feet away from them. Show your dog that you have some good treats in your hand. Say "Come," and clap your hands or slap your legs to get her excited about running toward you.

5. When she gets to you, say "Good come." Give her a treat and a good cuddle. Repeat this at least ten times.

6. Next, ask some friends and their dogs to walk around in your yard. Stand about ten feet from your dog. Show her you have treats. Say "Come" and clap your hands.

7. When she comes, say "Good girl" and give her a treat. If she doesn't come, pull her toward you by her leash. Give her a treat when she gets to you. Keep doing this until she comes to you.

8. Once your dog comes to you in your yard, teach her to come to you in other places. Practice in a park. Start from the beginning, including keeping her on leash, and go through each step at least ten times. Practice each step ten to twenty times for three or four days before moving to the next step.

9. Practice this every day. When you are out doing fun things, call her to come you and then give her a treat as a reward.

Leave It

Learning the *leave it* command will keep your dog from running after your cat, stop her from eating food off the floor, and keep her away from dangers on your walks. Here is how to teach your dog to leave it:

1. Show your dog that you have a piece of food in your hand. Don't let her take it. If she's pushy, ask a helper to hold her on leash.

2. Say "Leave it" but keep showing her the food. If she doesn't take it for a few seconds, say "Good leave it"

and give her the food. Have her wait for up to ten seconds between saying "Leave it" and giving her the treat. Do this ten to twenty times a day for three or four days.

3. Then put the food on the floor. Say "Leave it." Do not let your dog take the treat. Wait two seconds, and say "Take it." Now let her eat the treat. Increase the amount of time she has to wait. Do this ten to twenty times each day for three or four days.

Once your dog understands the *leave it* command, you can teach her to leave other things besides food. When she starts to chase the cat, pull her away by her leash, and say "Leave it." If she stops chasing, say "Good leave it" and give her a treat. On walks, say "Leave it" if she starts to sniff something you don't want her to. Pull her away, and say "Good leave it." Then give her a treat.

Walk on a Leash

Dogs that walk nicely on a leash get more walks and enjoy their walks more. If your dog pulls on the leash, you probably won't walk her as much. Pulling on the leash isn't much fun for your dog, either. It can even hurt her!

Teach your dog to walk nicely on a leash right from the start. For your dog's first walk, bring lots of treats. Start walking. If your dog pulls, stop. Turn around and walk in the other direction. When your pup catches up to you, give her a treat. Do this every time she pulls.

Start walking again. Hold your bag of treats at your hip in your left hand if your dog is on your left, and in your right hand if your dog is on your right. Be sure your dog sees the bag. She will probably look up at your hip as you walk. Give her a treat every once in a while. If she starts to walk ahead of you, stop. If she walks back to you, give her a treat from your treat bag and say "Good dog!" Repeat this walk-stop sequence several times.

Practice every day until she always walks nicely on her leash. Always bring treats on your walks. Be ready to stop whenever she starts pulling. If you make it only halfway down the block, don't worry. Keep training, and never let your dog get into the habit of pulling.

Naughty Things Dogs Do: Digging, Barking, and the Rest

We expect dogs to do all kinds of things that don't make much sense to them. We ask them not to dig up our gardens when they're trying to check out the good stuff buried there. We ask them not to bark at people when they're trying to protect us and their houses. We ask them not to eat food off our tables when they're just trying to keep their bellies full. They can learn to do what we like, though. Here's how to teach them.

Digging

Some dogs are born to dig. Terriers were bred for hundreds of years to dig after animals in underground burrows, so they're doing what comes naturally. Other dogs dig because they are bored. Don't leave your dog alone outside for long periods, and make sure he gets lots of exercise. This may end your digging problems.

If not, the best solution for a die-hard digger is to give him a digging spot of his own. A sandbox works well. Fill the sandbox with soft soil. In the soil, bury lots of your dog's favorite things such as toys, bones, or whatever he really loves. Show him the sandbox. Dig in it yourself to show that this is a prime digging spot. When he digs there, say "Good boy."

Barking

Dogs usually bark for a reason. They want to come in the house, they want to go outside, or they want some food. When dogs bark for no reason, it usually means they are bored. A dog that is left outside all

day or night will bark to keep himself busy. And if he doesn't get enough exercise, he will bark because he is anxious. It's easy to solve this kind of barking—bring your pup inside, and give him lots of exercise. Puzzle toys such as Kongs can help keep him busy.

Jumping Up

This habit is easier to prevent than to cure! When a puppy jumps up, people think it's cute. Everyone laughs and gives him kisses. He learns that jumping up is a good thing to do. When your puppy grows to be 50, 100, or 150 pounds and is still jumping up, no one will think it's

cute. It's easy to teach your puppy not to jump, but it's a lot harder to teach visitors not to let him jump!

To keep your dog from jumping up, get down to his level. Ask your visitors to squat down to greet your pup. Ignore your puppy if he jumps on you. Give him lots of praise and love when he stays on all four paws. If everyone does this, he'll quickly learn not to jump up. This works for older dogs, too.

Chewing

You can't teach dogs not to chew. You can teach a dog to chew on the right things, though.

Your dog has no idea what he can or cannot chew. He'll chew whatever looks good and is easiest to get to. Puppies like to chew things that smell like their people, such as shoes, wallets, remote controls, and eyeglasses.

To teach your pup what to chew and what not to chew, give him lots of his own safe dog toys. Don't let him chew on anything else. If you don't want some-

thing to be chewed, don't leave it out. If you leave your shoes out and he chews them, you have only yourself to blame. Soon, your dog will learn what are his toys and what are your toys.

Never give your dog old socks or shoes to chew on. This will teach him that these things are OK to chew. He can't tell the difference between a holey sock and a new one!

Nipping

Puppies use their teeth and mouths to explore the world, but those tiny needlelike teeth hurt.

Littermates and doggy moms teach puppies not to nip by yelping when a nip is too hard. You can do this, too. When your pup nips you, say "Ow!" Most

pups will be surprised enough to stop nipping for at least a moment or two.

Do this every time your pup nips, and soon he'll replace those nips with licks. If your puppy gets more excited when you yelp, stop playing with him. Let him calm down, and then start playing again. Stop the game whenever he nips. If he nips three times in a row, put him in his crate, and give him time to calm down. Do not scold him. This will only make him more excited. Sooner or later, he'll figure out that nipping means the fun ends. And no pup wants the fun to end!

Other Naughty Habits

There are many other naughty doggy habits. They include begging and getting on the furniture. You can keep bad habits from starting if you don't let your pup do them in the first place.

If you never give your dog food off your plate, your dog won't beg from you. Your dog should get all his food from his bowl.

A lot of people let puppies on furniture. When they grow into big, hairy, slobbery dogs, these people don't want them on the furniture anymore. If you don't want your adult dog on the couch, don't let your puppy on the couch. It's as simple as that. If your dog is never allowed on the couch, he probably won't get on the couch. It's when you change the rules that the trouble starts!

Now you know how to train your dog. Once he's trained, practice with him every day so he doesn't forget what he's learned. Teach him some new tricks as well to keep things interesting. And don't forget to have fun!

Retrieve Your **FREE** Subscription **TODAY!**